Miniature
Victorian
Lamps

Marjorie
Hulsebus

Schiffer Publishing Ltd

77 Lower Valley Road, Atglen, PA 19310

I dedicate this book to my husband, Paul, for his forbearance (T.V. dinners, phone bills, and sharing the household chores) in my endeavor to put this book together, and to my children, who have been very patient. I have not been able to see them as often as I would have liked while this project was underway.

Printed in Hong Kong
ISBN: 0-88740-931-8

Library of Congress Cataloging-in-Publication Data

Hulsebus, Marjorie.
    Miniature Victorian lamps/
    Marjorie Hulsebus.
        p. cm.
    Includes bibliographical references.
    ISBN 0-88740-931-8
    1. Miniature lamps--Collectors and collecting--Catalogs.
    I. Title.
    NK8475.L3H85   1996
    749'.63--dc20   96-3807
                        CIP

Published by Schiffer Publishing Ltd.
77 Lower Valley Road
Atglen, PA 19310
Please write for a free catalog.
This book may be purchased from the publisher.
Please include $2.95 postage.
Try your bookstore first.

Acknowledgments

Many years ago the thought of putting out a book on unlisted miniature lamps seemed like just another pipe dream. But while attending an auction in Fairfield, Maine, I presented the idea to Ruth Smith, a dear friend of mine. She, like many others since that time, encouraged me to pursue this thought. This book is the result. My intent is to picture as many previously unlisted lamps as possible, including variants of those in the books Ruth wrote with her husband Frank (in 1978) and independently (in 1982). Hereafter, I refer to these books as Smith I and Smith II.

None of this would have been possible without the cooperation of collectors all over the country. My gratitude to each and every one of you: Barbara B. Bridges; Carleton and Marion Cotting; Bob Culver; Peter Frenzel; Paul and Kathy Gresko, Spring City, PA; Jim and Joanne Gustin, Rockford, IL; Rick Hornwood, San Dimas, CA; Charles and Jane Knox, Mountain View Rd., Copake, NY 12516; David Lennox (Lennox/VanderMeer collection); Karen and Frank McWright, 21 Pell Mell, Bethel, CT; Dr. Richard C. Miller, 309 E. Main St., Ravenna, OH; Oldenlite II, P.O. Box 400, Concord, MA; Mr. and Mrs. Fred Reesbeck, River Vale, NJ; Chuck and Leona Rosenow, Rolla, MO; Bob and Pat Ruf; Dr. John Soverson, P.O. Box 428, Rochester, MI 48308; Charmaine Carry Trimble; Herb and Eileen White; Wendy Wharton; and Bill Young.

I'd like to thank Richard Miller for giving me the opportunity to purchase many of the beautiful lamps that appear in this book. Special thanks are given to Frank McWright for sharing his knowledge and time, answering my endless questions, and offering opinions when I most needed them. I owe him a debt of gratitude.

Contents

Introduction

This book provides a new view of miniature lamps, updated and expanded since Ruth Smith wrote *Miniature Lamps II* in 1982. Many exotic and unusual lamps have been discovered since then, and they are shown here for the first time. Pictures of most lamps from known manufacturers have already been published elsewhere, so it is reasonable to believe that the lamps pictured here represent the rarest and most unique forms of miniatures. It is hoped that this "study collection" will enhance the knowledge of miniatures, and provide the collector with a useful tool in evaluating and documenting these lamps.

"Knowledge is king," as they say, so it goes without saying that development of a good reference library is indispensable in the collection of miniature lamps. Other source materials, including the original *Miniature Lamps* by Frank R. and Ruth E. Smith, together with the *Value Guide For Miniature Lamps* by John F. Solverson, are an essential part of any collector's reference library, whether novice or experienced. The Smith Books are currently in print and available through Schiffer Publishing Company. Important information can also be found in other publications; some of them are out of print, but may still be available from book dealers in the decorative arts field. These include *Those Fascinating Little Lamps* by John F. Solverson, *Evolution Of The Night Lamp* by Ann McDonald (Wallace Homestead Book Co., Des Moines IA, 1979), *Victorian Miniature Oil Lamps* by Mrs. Edward J. Delmore (Forward Color Prod. Inc., Manchester VT, 1988), *Clarks Fairy Lamps* by Dorothy Tibbits, *19th Century Fairy Lamps* by T. Robert Anthony (Forward Clor Prod. Inc., Manchester VT, 1969), and *Fairy Lamps* by Amelia E. MacSwiggan. Other good references are past auction catalogs from major auction houses specializing in sales of miniature lamps, such as James D. Julia Inc. (P.O. Box 830, Fairfield ME 14937), or Bob, Chuck and Rich Roan Inc. (Box 118, R.D. #3, Cogan Station PA 17728).

In today's marketplace, collectors find it especially difficult to identify and locate correct examples. This fact, coupled with lack of information and rapidly escalating prices, makes the pursuit of miniature lamps both a difficult and sometimes risky process. Frequently, unknowledgable dealers will offer perfume bases or salt shakers with legitimate burners, and perhaps a shade or chimney, representing these items as a lamp. Similarly, dealers offer bases without shades, or with mismatched shades or a chimney, often suggesting to the unwary that the lamp is complete. Study the books! A good reference library is your best defense. In addition, to minimize these pitfalls, the collector should request a receipt stating the age and description of the lamp, and providing a guarantee of authenticity, completeness, and originality. At the same time, try to locate identical or similar examples in your reference material. By authenticating your purchases with the receipt and your own research, most mistakes can be limited, if not avoided entirely.

Even with good research and dealer assurances, some lamps are still difficult to authenticate. If major components are correct, i.e. base and shade, a replacement burner or chimney is acceptable. Often the correct burner or chimney is available in the marketplace. However, if the shade and base are of a different texture of glass, or of different coloration or embossing, the lamp is considered a mismatch, also referred to as a "marriage," and its value is substantially reduced.

The Value Guide for Miniature Lamps, referred to earlier, provides useful information in the evaluation of mismatches. In particular, the guide earmarks lamps that are reproductions or of questionable authenticity. This information is extremely valuable, since many old lamp styles of the 1890s vintage have been reproduced by L.G. Wright Company and Fenton Glass Company, using old molds or molds similar in appearance. Reprints of some of these styles are pictured here on pages 8 and 9.

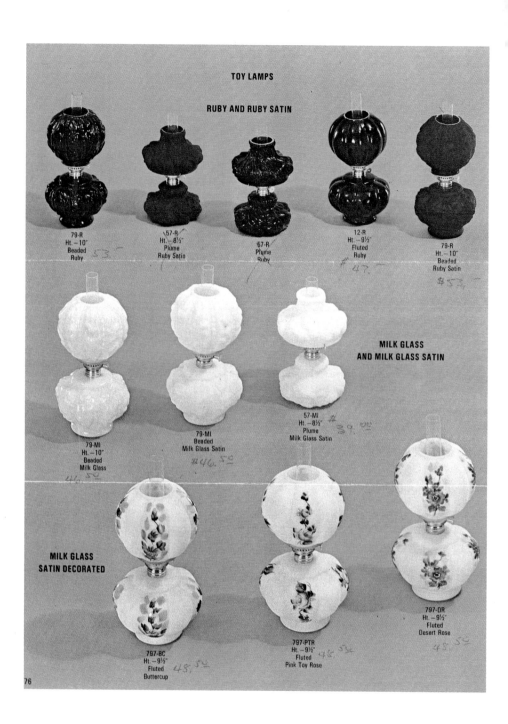

TOY LAMPS

RUBY AND RUBY SATIN

79-R
Ht. – 10"
Beaded
Ruby

57-R
Ht. – 8½"
Plume
Ruby Satin

57-R
Plume
Ruby

12-R
Ht. – 9½"
Fluted
Ruby

79-R
Ht. – 10"
Beaded
Ruby Satin

MILK GLASS AND MILK GLASS SATIN

79-MI
Ht. – 10"
Beaded
Milk Glass

79-MI
Beaded
Milk Glass Satin

57-MI
Ht. – 8½"
Plume
Milk Glass Satin

MILK GLASS SATIN DECORATED

797-BC
Ht. – 9½"
Fluted
Buttercup

797-PTR
Ht. – 9½"
Fluted
Pink Toy Rose

797-DR
Ht. – 9½"
Fluted
Desert Rose

DAISY & CUBE

79-AO
Height 10"
Beaded Satin
Amber/Overlay

57-AO
Height 8½"
Plume Satin
Amber/Overlay

45-AR
Height 10"

46-A
Height 10"

45-G
Height 10"

10-5
Height 9"
Cranberry Honeycomb

10-3
Height 9"
Cranberry Opal Dot
Also Available in
Cranberry Thumbprint

$76.50

11-6
Height 9"
Cranberry Honeycomb

11-3
Height 9"
Cranberry Opal Dot

11-1
Height 9"
Cranberry T.P.

$76.50

$76.50

MOON & STAR

44-B
Height 10"

44-A

$34.50

44-R

$34.50

$40.50

9

It is also important to note that there are numerous references in the Smith Books to lamp bases with variant shades. These are perfectly correct since the lamp was originally produced in a variety of forms. These examples are not to be confused with mismatches, and it is critical for the inexperienced collector to learn to differentiate between acceptable variations and mismatches. A review of the Smith Books will also provide useful information and pictures of variations shown in the catalog reprints. Once again, resort to the reference materials. They are your best protection.

Avoid bargains! Unless the price is nominal, resist the temptation to buy bases without the correct shade, hoping to find the right one later. It just doesn't happen! Don't let the high costs of good lamps and lack of availability push you into making a poor choice. It is a far better policy to save for a lamp you know is complete and correct.

Similarly, avoid the lure of the flea market in the hopes of finding complete miniature lamps at bargain prices. Sometimes this is more than the inexperienced collector can resist, but until you study the references, exercise an abundance of caution and certainly a strong degree of scepticism. Caveat emptor! After a number of years, collectors acquire a "gut feeling" about whether a lamp is correct or not, but this comes from years of experience and study, often resulting from lessons learned the hard way. My advice to the novice is to be prepared to sacrifice your investment in a prospective purchase if you are uncertain as to the authenticity of a lamp. The hunt is exciting and sometimes frustrating, but the pursuit of these elusive and beautiful little lamps is still worth the effort.

Finally, I encourage all collectors to share information and knowledge with other collectors. Network and join collector clubs such as the Night Light organization. The more we share, the more enjoyable the adventure. Happy lamping!

Opposite page, bottom:
The pictures shown here are examples of various lamp heights. Because it is difficult for inexperienced collectors to judge the height while looking at photographs, this may be of some help.

Firefly (Smith Book II #54) 4 1/2 in.
Firefly (Smith Book I #9) 6 in.
Cranberry (Smith Book II #477) 6 1/2 in.
Blue satinized shade (Smith Book I #258) 9 3/4 in.
Maroon/gold Nailsea (Smith Book I #582) 12 1/2 in.

The pictures shown here are examples of mismatches and marriages as described in the introduction.

1st example: Red satin base (Smith Book I #401) with red satin shade (Smith Book I #399).

2nd example: Yellow milk glass base (Smith Book I #221) with custard glass shade (Smith Book I #373).

3rd example: Blue milk glass base (Smith Book II #249) with blue milk glass shade (Smith Book I #212).

4th example: Brown painted milk glass base (Smith Book I #276) with unlisted brown painted milk glass shade.

About the Values

To compile a range of value estimates for the lamps in this book, I have asked for the help of contributing collectors. Keep in mind that if a lamp shown in this book has not been offered by dealers or been sold in auction houses more than once, it has no "track record" of steady pricing. These prices are provided in U.S. dollars, and reflect lamps in "mint condition." I sincerely hope that whoever uses this guide will understand that I am not trying to establish set prices for the lamps but merely to give an estimate of their market values at this time.

When you are actually out in the market, there are a great many factors involved in determining an appropriate value for a lamp. Among these factors are the current popularity trends, the rarity of the lamp, its condition and authenticity, and the location in the country where it was purchased. Often lamps purchased on the East Coast will command a higher price than those found on the West Coast; sometimes, however, the reverse is true.

Note: Lamps are numbered and described from left to right, unless otherwise noted.

Opposite page, bottom:
6. White milk glass finger lamp with fired-on flower decoration in aqua and orange. Tiny white milk glass shade. Olmsted burner. 4 1/4 in. Author's collection. $150

7. Tiny Dresden-type lamp with applied flower buds throughout stem and font. Blue, pink and gold decorative painting. Tiny burner marked Night Lamp. 5 in. to top of clear glass chimney. Author's collection. $200

8. Blue bristol glass base with painted flowers in cream, white and orange. White milk glass shade. Olmsted burner. 4 1/4 in. Author's collection. $150

9. Tiny silver finger lamp with elaborate Griffin-type handle. White milk glass ball shade with string wick protruding through the middle. "Meridan Silver Plate Co #3414" stamped on bottom. I believe this is a sealing wax lamp. 2 1/2 in. Author's collection. $200

THE LAMPS

1. Translucent blue glass with tin burner and reflector. Embossed "STAR LAMP" on the front and "E H" on the reverse side. 5 1/2 in. McWright collection. $85

2. Crystal "NIGHTWATCH" stem lamp with white milk glass chimney shade. Olmsted-type burner. 6 1/2 in. Knox collection. $175

3. Unsigned cobalt blue finger lamp with applied handle. Olmsted-type burner. White milk glass chimney shade. 4 1/2 in. Knox collection. $250

4. White opaline glass base and chimney shade both with enameled floral decor. Olmsted burner. 5 1/2 in. Knox collection. $175

5. "NOVELTY NIGHT LAMP" in light blue glass with tin burner and reflector. 6 in. Knox collection. $85

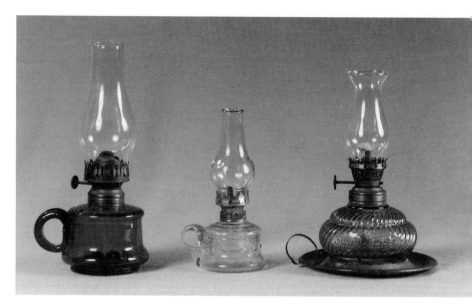

10. Reddish brown finger lamp. Applied handle. Hornet burner. 3 in. Gustin collection. $95

11. Clear glass finger lamp with embossed "SHIWI" and seven stars on the side. Acorn burner. 2 in. Gustin collection. $150

12. Blue glass saucer lamp with embossed swirls and the word "SUN LIGHT" on the side. Foreign burner. 3 in. Gustin collection. $135

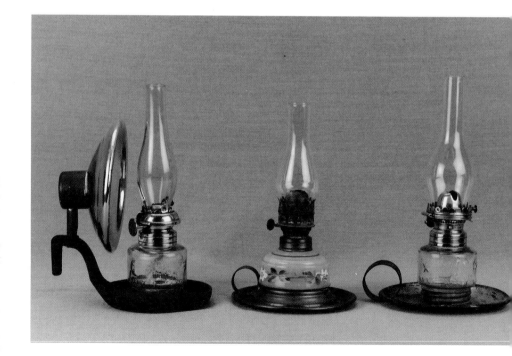

Opposite page, bottom:
13. French's Patent bracket lamp. Crystal font embossed with sun, moon and stars screwed into a cast iron holder with cast wall mount. 4 in. mercury glass reflector. Font signed "A. French's Pat July 5, 1870." Early burner. McWright collection. $500

14. Brass saucer lamp with light blue opalescent font enameled flowers and leaves. Nutmeg burner. 2 1/4 in. Reesbeck collection. $125

15. Crystal font embossed with sun, moon and stars. Also embossed "Pat July 5, 1870." Japanned tin saucer. Early burner. 2 7/8 in. One of a series of French's patent lamps. McWright collection. $125

16. Crystal finger lamp with applied handle. Font embossed "CONTINENTAL" with the outline of a shield below the word. Early burner 2 1/2 in. McWright collection. $175

17. Time lamp with same height and hour scale as Smith Book I #23, but no other markings. Smooth white milk glass shade. Thought to be the same lamp as pictured in the 1900 Butler Bros. catalog ad pictured on page 12 of Smith Book II. 6 1/2 in. McWright collection. $300

18. Crystal beehive pattern finger lamp with highly arched applied handle. Early burner. 2 1/4 in. McWright collection. $125

19. Crystal finger lamp embossed "LITTLE PEARL." Early burner. 2 7/8 in. McWright collection. $125

20. Plain crystal finger lamp with highly arched applied handle. Olmsted-type burner with white milk glass chimney shade. 4 3/4 in. McWright collection. $150

21. Amethyst finger lamp with embossed Greek Key design circling the bottom of the base. Acorn burner. 3 in. Hornwood collection. $125

22. White china figural head of Victorian lady with plumed bonnet, pink ribbon. Blue anchor marking on bottom. Nutmeg burner 3 1/2 in. to top of the collar. Author's collection. $225

23. Cobalt finger lamp with applied handle. Unmarked foreign burner. 2 1/2 in. to top of collar. Hornwood Collection. $125

24. Pink clear glass item depicting the head of George Washington. Embossing on each side "First in War"; "First in Peace." Bottom of base embossed Wheaton, N.J. Foreign burner. 3 1/2 in. to top of collar. Not old; not a lamp.

25. Blue finger lamp with harlequin design throughout. Applied handle. Incomplete foreign burner. 3 in. to top of collar. Author's collection. $125

Opposite page, bottom:

26. Green opaline glass with white milk glass chimney shade. Both pieces have enamelled floral decor. Olmsted burner. 5 in. Knox collection. $175

27. "LITTLE JIM" crystal font on a white milk glass foot. Milk glass shade. Olmsted-type burner. 5 1/2 in. Knox collection. $175

28. Blue opaline glass with a white chimney shade. Both pieces have enamelled decor. Olmsted-type burner. 5 3/4 in. Knox collection. $175

29. "IMPROVED LITTLE WONDER" in crystal with a white milk glass chimney shade. Olmsted-type burner. No finger holder. 4 3/4 in. Knox collection. $150

30. Blue milk glass fluted base with matching blue milk glass chimney shade. Foreign burner. 6 in. McWright collection. $350

31. Blue opaline lamp with green and white enamelled floral decor. White milk glass chimney shade. Olmsted burner. 3 7/8 in. McWright collection. $150

32. "ALLADIN LAMP" in crystal glass. No finger holder. Chinook burner. 3 in. Knox collection. $125

33. Cobalt blue " LITTLE HARRY'S NIGHT LAMP" with applied handle and matching chimney. Olmsted burner. 4 1/2 in. Variant of Smith Book I #13. Knox collection. $350

34. "IMPROVED LITTLE FAVORITE" in crystal glass with a white milk glass chimney shade. Olmsted-type burner. 7 1/4 in. Knox collection. $150

35. Plain crystal font with an Olmsted-type burner and a slightly elongated white milk glass chimney shade. 4 in. McWright collection. $100

36. Beehive pattern crystal stem lamp. Identical to Smith Book II #173 except for a small font (2 1/2 diameter) and Nutmeg fittings. 5 1/4 in. McWright collection. $100

37. Clear glass finger lamp embossed "SUN NIGHT LAMP" with sun rays embossed above the lettering. Narrow brass handle as shown in Smith Book I #29. Nutmeg burner. 2 3/4 in. White collection. $100

39. Cranberry finger lamp with internal diamond pattern. Clear applied handle. Not always found with cranberry chimney. Acorn burner. 2 1/2 in. to top of collar. Solverson collection. $250

40. Sapphire blue finger lamp with gold banding and white scroll design. Possibly Moser glass. White milk glass shade. Foreign burner. Not always found with milk glass shade. 2 1/2 in. to top of collar. Solverson collection. $150

38. Green milk glass finger lamp with panelled font and ribbed bottom. Brass handle similar to Smith Book I #29. Acorn burner. 2 1/2 in. Rosenow collection. $150

41. Tiny white milk glass finger lamp with matching chimney shade Multicolored floral decoration circling base and milk glass handle. Olmsted burner. 5 in. White collection. $150

42. Cobalt blue saucer lamp embossed "LITTLE HARRY'S NIGHT LAMP, L.H. Olmsted, New York." "Pat. Mar. 20, April 24, 1877" on the base of font. Brass tray is embossed "Pat. Nov. 6, '77." White shade embossed "L H." Tiny brass reflector is 1 1/4 in. diameter. A wishbone shaped spring-type clamp which is part of the handle holds the font in the tray. 3 1/2 in. (Also seen in teal and clear). White collection. $450

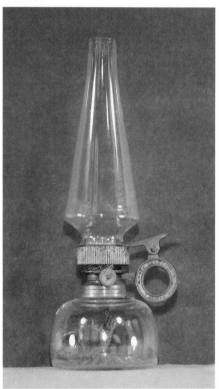

43. Clear glass lamp embossed "HELEN'S BABY." Tiny white milk glass shade. Olmsted burner. 3 3/4 in. Culver collection. $125

44. Clear glass finger lamp with applied handle embossed on the side "IMPERIAL CROWN." White milk glass shade. Olmsted burner. 5 1/2 in. Culver collection. $125

45. Clear glass lamp embossed "THE BOSS." Tiny white milk glass shade. Olmsted burner. 3 3/4 in. Culver collection. $125

46. Clear finger lamp with Tom Thumb burner. Circular finger ring is attached to the base of the burner. Burner marked "Tom Thumb," "Dirigo." Flanged chimney is attached to the burner by 3 flanges and a set screw. 3 1/2 in. to top of burner. Solverson collection. $300

47. Clear finger lamp with rope pattern and ribbing on top and bottom of lamp. Applied handle. Camphene pewter wick holder. 2 3/4 in. Rosenow collection. $200

48. Pale green lamp embossed "THE TRILBY NIGHT LAMP" with tin burner and reflector. Back of lamp embossed "Pat. applied For." 5 1/2 in. Solverson collection. $85
49. Inverted hobnail finger lamp with clear applied handle. Pewter collar and stem burner. 2 1/2 in. Solverson collection. $150

50. Lavender opaline glass with enameled white floral decor and gold trim bands. Olmsted burner with white milk glass chimney shade. 4 1/4 in. McWright collection. $150

51. White milk glass stem lamp embossed "LITTLE VISTA ERATICATOR." Olmsted-type burner with white milk glass chimney shade. 6 in. McWright collection. $150

52. Emerald green bead and panel pattern. Paneled chimney is the same as found on S2-225. Elongated neck on base with vertical beading separating each panel. Acorn burner. 7 in. McWright collection. $195

53. Delicate white milk glass decorated with pink, lavender and green floral designs. Embossed ribbing at top and bottom of ball shade and at top of the base. Nutmeg burner. 7 in. McWright collection. $250

54. Greenish opaline glass with enameled floral decor. Olmsted burner and white milk glass chimney shade also floral decorated. 5 1/2 in. McWright collection. $175

55. Tiny silver cigar lighter with striker, snuffer and marked "Derby Silver Co" on bottom. 5 1/4 in. Author's collection. $200

56. Delft-type lamp of white milk glass; boat scene in shade and base. (I feel that this is a correct version of Smith Book I, #338; also see Smith II, #353.) Foreign burner. 6 in. Author's collection. $275

57. Pewter embossed base with plum colored satin shade. Small unmarked foreign burner. 6 in. Author's collection. $200

58. White milk glass pedestal-type lamp with blue lines circling base; colorful flowers of pink; leaves of green and yellow. Unmarked foreign burner. 6 in. Author's collection. $250

59. White Bristol glass lamp with decorations in red and gold. White opalescent shade. Olmsted-type burner. 4 in. Author's collection. $150

60. White milk glass pedestal lamp with the word "MATCHLESS" embossed on the font. White milk glass shade. Olmsted burner. 6 3/4 in. Solverson collection. $200

61. White Bristol pedestal-type base. Shade fits on tripod affixed to foreign burner. 9 in. Author's collection. $250

62. Amber optic ribbed font on an amber stem. Acorn burner. 4 5/8 in. This is the US Glass version of a lamp originally made by Hobbs Glass. The Hobbs version had a matching shade. This lamp is pictured in the US Glass catalog reprint in Thuro's first volume, page 329. Also found in crystal and blue. McWright collection. $200

63. Crystal optic ribbed base with matching shade. Nutmeg burner. 7 1/2 in. This lamp is pictured in a Hobbs Glass ad reprinted in McDonald's Book page #75. It was subsequently sold as a stem lamp,

following the merger of Hobbs into US glass. McWright collection. $450

64. Amber stem lamp with optic ribbed pattern. Hornet sized burner. 6 in. Also found in blue and crystal McWright collection. $175

65. Six panel diamond hatch pattern in amber glass. Hornet burner. 5 1/2 in. Also found in crystal. McWright collection. $175

66. Blue glass stem lamp in the Pickett pattern. Acorn Burner. 5 in. This is the stemmed version of Smith Book I #46. Also found in crystal. McWright collection. $175 in blue; $125 in clear glass.

67. Clear stem lamp with ribbed panelled umbrella shaped font. Embossed fan pattern on the base. 5 1/4 in. Solverson collection. $100

68. Cranberry opalescent reverse swirl pattern with brass foot. Complete as is. Nutmeg burner. 4 in. Also found in blue, vaseline and crystal. Pictured in Butler Bros. 1890 catalog. McWright collection. $300 in cranberry; $150 in clear glass.

69. Clear glass stem lamp with reverse-embossed strawberries and leaves around bottom of base, highlighted by gold and red paint. 6 in. Culver Collection. $100

70. Westward Ho stem lamp; frosted font depicting a bison, deer and log cabin. This patterned glass was made in serving pieces. However, the lamp wasn't made until many years later. Hornet burner. 6 in. Author's collection. $350

71. Frosted stem lamp called "Dakota Night Lamp" by the National Glass Co. in their catalog dated 1901. Nutmeg burner. 5 1/2 in. Author's collection. $175

72. Pink and white spatter stem lamp referred to as the "Bloxam" lamp in Thuros' Book II, page #104. 4 1/2 in. Author's collection. $275

73. Clear glass with embossed bands forming panels. Each shade panel has an embossed cat face. Paint on embossed bands badly worn. Similar to Smith book 1 #138. Hornet burner. 8 in. Reesbeck collection. $200

74. Clear glass lamp with red and blue enamelled flowers on pedestal base and chimney shade. (Thought to be a perfume lamp). 7 in. Oldenlite II collection. $200

75. Metal pedestal lamp with clear font and white chimney shade. Foreign burner. 6 1/2 in. Oldenlite II collection. $200

76. Crystal finger lamp with matching half shade. Advertised by Imperial Glass as pattern #9; the shade being optional. Hornet burner. 7 1/2 in. Although heavily reproduced in many colors, the original lamp was only made in crystal and crystal has not been reproduced to date. McWright collection. $275

Opposite page:
77. Clear stem-type lamp with shade. Both shade and base have a matching engraved decor. Nutmeg burner. 8 1/2 in. Solverson collection. $375

Opposite page:
78. Clear glass "Nellie Bly"-type lamp with etched flowers and leaves. Hornet burner. 9 in. Author's collection. $150

79. Clear glass shade and base with gold paint highlighting ribbed top of base and shade. The base is the same as Smith Book I #165. I believe this lamp to be correct. Hornet burner. 6 3/4 in. Rosenow collection. $295

80. "LITTLE HARRY'S BRACKET LAMP" with cobalt blue font and shade. Flying saucer shaped font embossed "Little Harry's Night Lamp." Olmsted burner. A very rare variant of Smith Book I #14. McWright collection. $1,200

81. "EVENING STAR" bracket lamp in crystal with white milk glass chimney shade. Olmsted-type burner. Font has a raised bead around the middle to keep it level in the bracket ring. Ring is larger than Smith Book II #53. McWright collection. $650

Opposite page,
top and bottom left:
82. Crystal "LITTLE LILLY" bracket lamp with white milk glass chimney shade. Olmsted-type burner. Knox collection. $600

Opposite page,
top and bottom right:
83. Bracket lamp with blue glass flying saucer shaped font and white milk glass chimney shade. Orange and white enameled floral decor. Olmsted-type burner. Knox. collection. $600

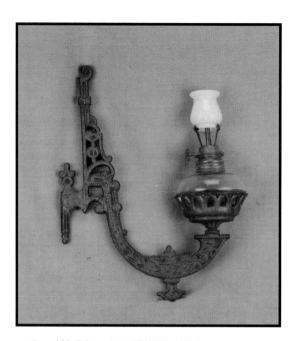

84. Wall bracket "FIREFLY" lamp. Bracket arm is identical to that shown in Firefly chandelier in Smith Book I #8 with embossed font and Olmsted burner. Tiny milk glass shade. 3 3/4 in. from base of font to top of shade. Author's collection. $700

85. Wall bracket "NIGHT WATCH" lamp. Iron bracket gilded gold with white milk glass font embossed in blue with red band circling font shoulder. White milk glass shade. Olmsted burner. 4 1/4 in. Also found with clear glass font and white milk glass shade. Author's collection. $650

86. Gilded iron wall bracket lamp with ornate Liberty head. White milk glass font and shade. Foreign burner. Similar to Smith Book I #91. 7 1/2 in. Author's collection. $350

87. Porcelain clock face which uses a small lamp or gas jet to illuminate the dial which measures 6 in. No visible date on the clock. See Smith Book II #311. Author's collection. $375

Left:
88. Brass "SCHERING'S FORMA-LIN LAMP" with glass tubular chimney and brass cup which held pastils used for deodorization, prevention of contagious diseases and preservation of foods. Foreign burner. 7 1/4 in. Author's collection. $125

Below:
90. Ribbed brass hanging glow lamp. Glass burner with teal blue shade. Complete paper label on rear of tank reads "Electric Glow Lamp." 7 3/4 in. McWright collection. $175

91. Brass finger lamp with swirled ribbed white milk glass shade and clear chimney. Burner signed "Luna FS & Co." 5 in. McWright collection. $100

92. Illuminated travel clock. Brass lighthouse shape with 1 1/2 diameter white milk glass shade. Black numerals on shade. Clock mechanism in base turns font and shade past fixed time pointer. 2 1/4 in. diameter wooden platform at bottom detaches and holds clock key. Brass cover fits over lamp for travel. 5 1/4 in. McWright collection. $1,500

93. French's patented warmer. Clear font with cable embossing screwed to a cast iron fingered holder and warmer plate. Font signed "Patd. June 5, 1870." String burner. 5 5/8 in. McWright collection. $175

Above:
89. Brass traveling lamp with black carrying case. Foreign burner. 7 in. Lamp can be raised on rod. The end of the rod fits into a hole in the lid or the black case to hold in position. Embossed label reads "James How & Co; 73 Farrinon St., London." Rosenow collection. $325

94. Brass skater's lantern. Cone signed "Patd. Dec. 24, 1867." Thumb wheel signed " Hurricane Lattern Co.." 9 in. McWright collection. $275

95. Large brass skater's lamp with ball handle. Cone signed "Patd. Dec. 24, 1867." Globe signed "5 April 1864." 9 3/8 in. McWright collection. $300

96. Large brass skater's lamp with wire globe guard. Originally a presentation piece with the globe engraved "C. Wallace." Cone signed "Patd. Dec. 24, 1867." 10 in. McWright collection. $400

97. Large brass skater's lamp with wire globe guard. Guard signed "March 24, 1874." Globe signed "5 April 1964." 10 in. McWright collection. $300

98. Brass skater's lamp. Cone signed "Patd. Dec. 24, 1867." 9 1/2 in. McWright collection. $275

99. Brass skater's lattern with question mark handle. Cone signed "Patd. Dec. 24, 1867." 7 1/4 in. McWright collection. $275

Opposite page:
100. Stars and Bars cigar lighter in crystal glass. Pet Ratchet burner. 8 3/4 in. McWright collection. $500

101. Brass lion's head cigar lighter lamp with two ornate strikers. Center matching filler cover. 4 in. Rosenow collection. $200

Opposite page:
102. Brass student lamp with two-part milk glass illuminator and shade. Similar to Smith book I #83 and Bristol Brass ad Smith Book II #295. Fiery milk glass illuminator is embossed "Pat. Dec. 26, '76; Pat. Mch 13, '77 Reis: Pat. April 24, '77 Reis." Unmarked burner. Base to top of ring 8 1/4 in. White collection. $1,200

103. Admiral Dewey lamp. Bullet shaped base embossed with lettering and shape of a ship. Crossed cannons support lamp. White Bristol ball shade with hand painted scene of ship at sea. P/A Victor burner. 12 in. Ruf collection. $1,000

104. Decorative etched brass footed base with drop in font. Green milk glass ball shade. Foreign burner. 8 3/4 in. Gresko Collection. $250

105. Metal hanging and carrying lamp with blue font. Frosted shade may or may not be original. Vienna burner. 6 in. Rosenow collection. $100

106. Brass student lamp. Similar to Kleeman Student lamp by C.F.A. Heinrich Co. White milk glass floral decorated shade. Measures 12 1/4 in. from base to top of center post. Shade is old but not original. Foreign burner. Solverson collection. $1,200

107. Brass pedestal lamp with Greek Key design outlining base and shade. Unique tripod holds jeweled shade with green fringe. Foreign burner. 10 in. Culver collection. $125

108. Aqua satin glass lamp with pedestal-type base and ball shade. Foreign burner. 8 1/2 in. Author's collection. $250

109. White milk glass lamp with cupid scene on the base and ball shade. Foreign burner. 10 in. Hornwood collection. Lamp of questionable vintage. $200

110. Blue milk glass lamp with decal of strawberries in red, gold leaves and white stems. White dots circle bottom of base and shoulder of lamp. Foreign burner. 9 in. Author's collection. $250

Note: I feel that the last two lamps are not period lamps, but are still worth identifying in this book. Several other lamps later in the book are not period lamps, and are identified as such.

111. Cobalt blue embossed lamp with white coralene flowers on base and shade. Gold highlighting throughout. Foreign burner. 8 3/4 in. Author's collection. See Smith Book II #458. $250

112. Cobalt blue Mary Gregory-type lamp with fine overshot on pedestal-type base. Ball shade with white fired on paint. Foreign burner. 9 in. Author's collection. Another lamp example of questionable vintage. $400

113. White satin glass embossed lamp with blue and pink flowers and green leaves. Foreign burner. 8 3/4 in. See Smith Book II #458. Bridges collection. $250

114. Spatter glass shade and base with white background and colors of blue, orange and rust. Chimney globe shade. I don't believe this lamp is old but worthy of showing in this category. Acorn burner. 8 in. Gustin collection. $150

115. I would like to share this picture of a stained glass lamp hanging ornament in memory of a dear friend and fellow miniature lamp collector, Nedra Lennox, who passed away in January of 1994. Her husband, Franklin, made a number of these stained glass ornaments for Nedra to give as gifts to friends. I miss her love and friendship.

116. Light blue lamp with pedestal-type base and chimney globe shade. Found in various colors. This is not an old lamp. 10 in. Solverson collection. $150

117. Deep raspberry to pink satin DQMOP lamp with frosted applied feet. Nutmeg burner. Also found in yellow. This lamp is judged to have been made in the l930s or 1940s era. 10 in. Solverson collection. $300

118. White milk glass lamp with poorly fired on paint of a black sword, green leaves and red flower. "Eucharistic Congress Ireland 1932 God Bless our Home." Unmarked foreign burner. 6 1/2 in. $135

119. Green glass embossed beading on base with fluted embossing on shade. May or may not be original. (See Smith Book II #220.) Acorn burner. 6 3/4 in. Author's collection. $125

120. White milk glass finger lamp with applied milk glass handle. Utilitarian milk glass shade. Unmarked pewter fittings. 7 1/2 in. Author's collection. $125

121. Green glass lamp with scroll design on base and faintly panelled shade. Foreign burner. 7 in. Author's collection. $150

122. Blue glass lamp with embossed base and shade as shown in Smith Book II #226. One piece collar and burner made of tin which slips over neck of base. No markings. 5 3/4 in. McWright collection. $175

123. Cranberry glass variation of Smith book II #226. No finger holder. Tin collar and burner signed "DRGM." 5 3/4 in. McWright collection. $225

124. Small amethyst base and shade. Foreign burner. 5 in. Young collection. $175

125. Blue base and shade slightly different from amethyst lamp. Foreign burner. 5 in. Young collection. $175

126. White milk glass lamp with embossed design. Fan and flower decor in shades of blue and brown. Nutmeg burner. 7 1/4 in. Similar to Smith Book I #247 but different base. Cotting collection. $325

127. Butterscotch opaque with slag effect. Both shade and base are embossed with six divided panels with an Iris design embossed in every other panel. Made by New Martinsville Glass, W.VA. Hornet burner. 8 1/4 in. White collection. $400

128. White milk glass lamp with Greek Key design circling base and shade. Top of base and shade has worn yellow/gold paint. Hornet burner. 9 in. Solverson collection. $150

129. White satin glass lamp with ribbed and embossed design on base and shade. Nutmeg burner. 8 in. Oldenlite II collection. $425

130. Green milk glass lamp with embossed panels. Smith Book I #202. Hornet burner. 8 1/4 in. Reesbeck collection. $350

131. Milk glass lamp painted soft yellow. Embossed scrolls and leaves highlighted in gold. Acorn burner. 8 in. Reesbeck collection. $285

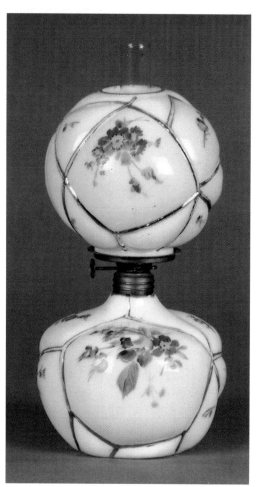

132. Blown out milk glass wrapped in gold cording. Hand painted flowers in orange and pink. Acorn burner. 9 in. Ruf collection. $375

133. Milk glass lamp with blue ground. Commemorative lamp with "Cleveland" and "1892" decorating the base and shade. See Smith Book II #252 for companion lamp. Glass shade holder. Hornet burner. 9 1/4 in. Solverson collection. $595

134. White satin glass shading to blue on top of shade and base. Orange and light green coralene decorations. Nutmeg burner. 8 in. Lennox/VanderMeer collection. $325

135. Milk glass lamp with lime green ground and darker green decoration of circles and bands. Three small enameled leaf designs outlined in yellow around base. Foreign burner 9 in. Gustin Collection. $350

136. White milk glass lamp with rose and white floral decor; green leaves. Foreign burner, 10 1/2 in. Lennox/VanderMeer collection. $350

137. Milk glass lamp with light blue ground; large flowers painted rose with yellow and green centers; large aqua leaves. Ruffled butterfly shade. Foreign burner. 9 1/4 in. Lennox/VanderMeer collection. $385

138. Yellow ground painted Bristol glass lamp with rust colored leaves and flowers. Foreign burner. 9 3/4 in. Author's collection. $350

139. Green painted ground with fired on garland of flowers and leaves in white and cream. Similar to Smith Book I #601. Nutmeg burner. 8 1/2 in. Author's collection. $325

140. White milk glass with yellow painted ground; brown stems, green leaves and bright orange flowers. Nutmeg burner. 8 1/2 in. Author's collection. $350

141. Opaque colored lamp with confetti-type overshot. This is the same lamp as shown in Smith Book II #214. Hornet burner. 9 1/2 in. Author's collection. $250

142. Satinized white milk glass lamp with embossed ribbing. Yellow and green floral decor with rust trim bands. Nutmeg burner. 7 7/8 in. Thought to be of Gillinder manufacture due to its close resemblance to Smith Book I #393. McWright collection. $375

143. Delft decorated porcelain base and porcelain shade. Foreign burner. 9 1/4 in. Base as shown in Smith Book II #418. McWright collection. $600

144. Delft decorated porcelain base and white milk glass shade. Foreign burner. Base signed "L." 8 in. McWright collection. $425

145. White milk glass lamp with embossed shell pattern on shade and base. Blue and yellow floral decor. Pink trimmed bands at top of shade and base. Nutmeg burner. 7 in. The base of this lamp was used as the base for Smith Book I #270. McWright collection. $350

146. Green satinized glass lamp with enamel white floral decoration on both shade and base. Foreign burner. 7 1/2 in. Oldenlite II collection. $375

147. White milk glass with embossed base and shade. Foreign burner. 7 3/4 in. Oldenlite II collection. $250

148. Painted "gold" glass lamp with floral decorations on both shade and base in deep orange flower motif. Foreign burner. 6 3/4 in. Oldenlite II collection. $325

149. Aqua bristol glass lamp with fired on painted flowers in orange and white; leaves of green and gray paint. Foreign burner. 8 in. Author's collection. $350

150. Blue milk glass lamp with ribbed swirled design. Square base and ball shade ribbing outlined in gold. Foreign burner. 9 1/2 in. Author's collection. $425

151. Blue bristol glass pedestal-type lamp with white flowers circling the shade and base; gold highlighting decoration. Foreign burner. 8 in. Author's collection. $350

152. Bristol glass lamp with painted decoration in red and blue with orange banding at top and foot of the base. Matching ball shade. Foreign burner. 7 1/2 in. Oldenlite II collection. $350

153. Pink cased glass lamp with enameled floral decoration in blue, white, and green. Foreign burner. 9 1/2 in. Knox collection. $500

154. White opaline glass lamp. Pink ground with black trim lines. Orange, blue and gray floral decor. Foreign burner. 6 3/4 in. McWright collection. $325

155. Pink opaline glass with spattering decoration in bright red, orange and brown. Foreign burner. 7 1/4 in. Author's collection. $375

156. Purple Bristol glass with hand painted flowers of blue and orange; green leaves. Bands of red outlining pedestal-type base. Foreign burner. 8 1/2 in. Author's collection. $500

157. White milk glass painted orange; black bands outline shade and base; flowers in orange and purple. Small foreign burner. 6 1/2 in. Author's collection. $325

158. Ruby cut to clear glass, Bohemian-type lamp, design identical in both shade and base. A correct version of Smith II #414. Acorn burner.   7 1/2 in. Author's collection. $300

159. Amber glass lightly panelled base with slightly embossed floral design chimney globe shade. Acorn burner. 6 1/2 in. Author's collection. $275

160. Deep blue embossed base with fired on painted windmill scene. Panelled ball shade with same scene. Foreign burner. 6 1/4 in. Author's collection. $375

161. Cranberry conical shaped base and shade with deep inverted swirl design. Foreign burner. 5 1/4 in. Author's collection. $425

162. Green glass faintly panelled lamp with fired on white painted flowers and leaves. Also found in cranberry and amber. Foreign burner. 5 in. Author's collection. $450 in green; $500 in cranberry

163. Small cranberry lamp with rectangular base embossed on four sides. Ball shade has gold enamel design. 5 1/2 in. Duris collection. $425

164. Green glass faintly panelled lamp with white enameled flowers and orange center. Foreign burner. 6 in. Young collection. $425

165. Midnight blue panelled lamp with white flower decoration on shade and base. Upturned ruffled shade. Foreign burner. 9 3/4 in. Ruf collection. $800

166. Aqua green glass lamp with large diamond pattern in shade and base. Shade has scalloped petal effect at the top. Foreign burner. 9 1/4 in. Ruf collection. $425

167. Blue clear glass hexagonal shaped lamp with hexagon design on base and shade. Foreign burner. 7 in. Ruf collection. $425

168. Lime green glass, slightly panelled with clusters of orange and
white dots on shade and base. Foreign burner. Similar to Smith Book I
#472. Also found in amber. 6 in.
Author's collection. $425

169. Rubina textured glass with
painted colorful flower design on upturned ruffled shade and base. Foreign burner. 7 3/4 in. Author's collection. $650

170. Green glass with fired on gold
gilt for leaves and stems; small pink
rosebuds on shade and base. Foreign burner. 5 1/2 in. Author's collection. $450

171. Clear irodized glass shading
to lavender on bottom of base and
top of ruffled shade. Hand painted
stag in natural colors; green shrubs.
Foreign burner. 8 1/2 in. Author's
collection. $675

172. Clear glass lamp with pink frosted bands at bottom and top of base and shade. White enamel flowers; blue dots with red centers. 7 1/2 in. Foreign burner. Lennox/VanderMeer collection. $425

173. Textured lamp in colors of gray to green with center portion having rust and green leaves outlined in gold. Foreign burner. 7 in. Cotting collection. $425

174. Green and orange satinized paint over clear glass lamp. Green, red and yellow fired on decorations. Base dimpled on 4 sides. Foreign burner. 9 in. Author's collection. $325

175. Light blue satinized lamp with panelled design; upturned ruffled shade. One large colorful pansy of purple and cream with orange center. Foreign burner. 8 in. Author's collection. $375

176. Peach Bristol glass lamp with large painted purple pansy, green leaves, gold banding on upturned ruffled shade. Foreign burner. 9 in. Author's collection. $375

177. White milk glass painted a pale cream color. Blue, pink and maroon floral decor with enamelled highlights. Foreign burner. 8 in. McWright collection. $350

178. Green milk glass base and shade with enamelled pink and white flowers set against a dark green band on base and shade. Garlands of green festoon both pieces. Foreign burner. 9 in. McWright collection. $375

179. White milk glass with burgundy, blue and green floral decor. Yellow trim bands at top of shade and upper and lower portion of base. Foreign burner. 9 1/2 in. Knox collection. $375

180. Clear glass painted a pale green in a matte finish. Blue, green and red decor. Foreign burner. 9 in. A variation of Smith Book I #344. McWright collection. $350

181. Bristol glass, soft lime green ground with hand painted pink and green flowers. Gold banding on base and upturned ruffled shade. Nutmeg burner. 10 in. Author's collection. $425

182. Tomato red cased shade and base with heavy embossed design depicting owls on the base and butterflies on the shade. Unusual reed and scroll embossing throughout lamp. Foreign burner. 9 1/2 in. Author's collection. $475

183. Bristol glass with blue and cream painted ground. Hand painted flowers in maroon with green leaves. Gold and maroon banding. Foreign burner. 9 3/4 in. Author's collection. $425

184. Brightly colored milk glass lamp with orange decor, blue flowers and green vine. (Possibly a variant of Smith Book I #355.) Foreign burner. 9 in. Author's collection. $325

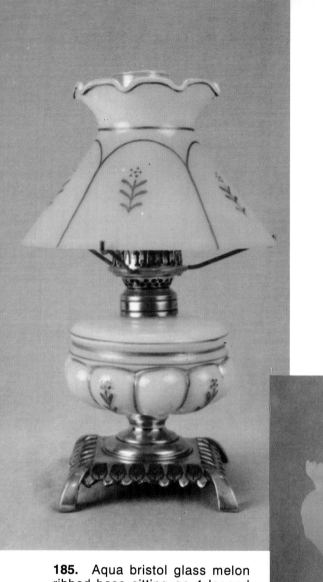

185. Aqua bristol glass melon ribbed base sitting on 4 legged brass pedestal base. Umbrella shade fluted at the top. Gold leaf design on shade and base. May or may not be original. Hornet burner. 10 in. Author's collection. $400

186. Blue milk lamp with ridged swirl and large embossed flower on shade and base. Upturned fluted shade. Foreign burner. 9 in. Gresko collection. $800

187. Brass pedestal lamp with separate shade ring riser. Oil cap marked "Carl Holy Berlin." Bristol globe-of-the-world shade. Foreign burner. 9 1/2 in. Author's collection. $275

188. Blue mottled porcelain handled base; lavender and orange pansy flowers, green leaves . Lamp outlined with white dots on shade and base. Foreign burner. 9 1/2 in. Author's collection. $300

189. Iridized glass lamp with green bands at top of shade and bottom of base. Fired on paint of pink, white and gold floral and scroll design. Foreign burner. 7 1/2 in. Author's collection. $375

190. Brass pedestal lamp with pink cased ribbed shade which fits onto separate shade ring riser. Separate oil cap. Foreign burner. 10 in. Author's collection. $350

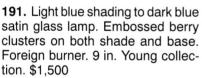

191. Light blue shading to dark blue satin glass lamp. Embossed berry clusters on both shade and base. Foreign burner. 9 in. Young collection. $1,500

192. Pink glossy lamp with ball shade. Foreign burner. 8 1/2 in. Young collection. $500

193. Blue glass satin finish lamp with heavy geometric embossed design. Foreign burner. 8 1/4 in. Young collection. $800

194. Pink cased pedestal lamp with the top edge of the shade in a scalloped design. Foreign burner. 9 1/4 in. Oldenlite II collection. $425

195. Pale pink satin glass lamp with large embossed daisies and leaves on shade and base. Foreign burner. 8 in. Reesbeck collection. $450
196. Blue clear glass hand lamp with embossed design on base and shade. Foreign burner. 7 in. Oldenlite II collection. $475

197. Pink cased pedestal lamp with decor of white flowers and green leaves. Foreign burner. 9 in. Bridges collection. $475

198. Sapphire blue glass lamp with white enameled floral decor and gold highlighting. Foreign burner. 9 1/2 in. McWright collection. $800

199. Clear opalescent reverse swirl pattern mounted on a brass font. Nutmeg burner. 7 1/4 in. This lamp is pictured in the 1890 Butler Bros. catalog. McWright collection. $1,200

200. Cranberry opalescent windows pattern mounted on a brass base. Nutmeg burner. 7 1/4 in. An identically shaped lamp in the Reverse Swirl pattern is pictured in the 1890 Butler Bros. catalog. McWright collection. $1,500

201. Blue clear glass double handled lamp with matching chimney and shade embossed with wide vertical ribbing. Acorn burner 8 1/4 in. Oldenlite II collection. $1,500

202. Rose iridescent wide panelled lamp with white cluster of flower design; gold leaves and decoration on upturned ruffled shade. Foreign burner. 8 in. Author's collection. $500

203. Green glass lamp, iridized finish, heavy gold decoration of grapes and leaves. Upturned ruffled shade. Foreign burner. 9 in. Author's collection. $425

204. Midnight blue honeycomb pattern lamp with upturned ruffled shade. Foreign burner. 9 3/4 in. Author's collection. $475

205. Honey colored reverse swirl lamp, flared out chimney globe shade. This lamp also found in blue, and overshot pink. Hornet burner. 8 1/4 in. Author's collection. $700

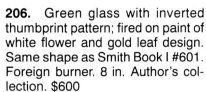

206. Green glass with inverted thumbprint pattern; fired on paint of white flower and gold leaf design. Same shape as Smith Book I #601. Foreign burner. 8 in. Author's collection. $600

207. Green glass lightly panelled shade and base with geometric fired on design of squares and flowers, long yellow stems. Foreign burner. Also found in clear frosted with floral design. 8 in. Author's collection. $350

208. Emerald green lamp, faintly panelled with ball shade. No decoration. Foreign burner. 8 in. Author's collection. $300

209. Green glass shade and base; white fired on leaf design with blue and orange centers. Nutmeg burner. 8 in. Author's collection. $600

210. Cranberry glass lamp decorated with white enamel paint. Lilly of the Valley Flowers on both base and shade. Foreign burner. 7 1/2 in. Oldenlite II collection. $600

211. Cranberry glass lamp with clear applied feet. Ball-type shade. Acorn burner. 7 1/4 in. Oldenlite II collection. $700

212. Cranberry glass lamp with Mary Gregory-type decoration of a boy and girl chasing butterflies. Nutmeg burner. 8 1/4 in. McWright collection. $850

213. Cranberry glass lamp with matching embossed base and shade. Foreign burner. 7 1/4 in. Oldenlite II collection. $500

214. Cranberry glass lamp with wide ribbing in shade and base. Light gold tracings. Nutmeg burner. 9 in. Oldenlite II collection. $425

215. Green satin shade mounted on a glossy green translucent base. Red and gold floral trim on both. Hornet burner. 9 3/4 in. A variant of Smith Book I #258. Also found in blue. Knox collection. $285

216. Cranberry glass lamp with clear applied handle. Beaded and ribbed embossed design on base and shade. Hornet burner. 9 in. Oldenlite II collection. $500

217. Cranberry panelled lamp with enamel design on both shade and base. Upturned ruffled shade slightly different from the next lamp. Foreign burner. 10 in. Lennox/VanderMeer collection. $600

218. Cranberry glass lightly pan-elled with intricate hand painted white flowers and geometric design. Upturned scalloped shade. Foreign burner. 10 in. Author's collection. $600

219. Green glass with white painted flowers and gold band on base and shade. Top of shade scalloped.

Similar to Smith Book I #459. Foreign burner. 9 3/4 in. Author's collection. $600

220. Cranberry glass with intricate hand painted white geometric design and gold bands. Upturned ruffled shade. Foreign burner. 9 1/2 in. Hornwood collection. $600

221. Blue glass lamp with artichoke-type embossing on both shade and base. Foreign burner 7 in. Lennox/VanderMeer collection. $425

222. Cranberry lamp heavily embossed with flowers and leaves. Foreign burner. 6 3/4 in. Lennox/VanderMeer collection. $475

223. Transparent blue ribbed swirl lamp. Base has four sides; shade is six-sided. Foreign burner. 7 3/4 in. Lennox/VanderMeer collection. $525

224. Blue embossed finger lamp with matching shade; applied handle. Foreign burner. 6 3/4 in. Author's collection. $425

225. Cranberry embossed finger lamp with matching shade; applied clear glass handle. Foreign burner. 6 1/2 in. Hornwood collection. $425

226. Blue satin embossed lamp with slight gold decoration still remaining. Foreign burner. 7 in. Author's collection. $400

227. Cranberry lamp with wide swirled panels in pedestal-type base. Upturned ruffled shade has smaller panelling with swirled effect. Foreign burner. 7 in. Author's collection. $500

228. Cranberry font on clear short pedestal base. Cranberry chimney globe shade. Foreign burner. 9 3/4 in. Ruf collection. $500

229. Cranberry glass heavily panelled in both the base and umbrella shade. Nutmeg burner. 7 1/4 in. Author's collection. $575

230. Ruby red etched lamp with forest scene, animals and scroll design. Hornet burner. 9 1/2 in. Author's collection. $300

231. Tall green pedestal lamp with goblet-type base and chimney globe shade. I feel that this lamp is old. Foreign burner. 12 1/2 in. Author's collection. $225

232. Ruby red colored lamp slightly panelled. Hornet burner. 8 1/2 in. Author's collection. $325

233. Cream colored floral decorated porcelain base with an acid etched floral decorated crystal shade tinted green. Foreign burner. 8 in. McWright collection. $400

234. Cranberry glass lamp with fired on decoration in white and blue accented with gold. Hornet burner. 9 1/4 in. Reesbeck collection. $500

235. Bisque court jester dressed in blue stepping from between light pink curtains. Straw colored foot. Blue cased floral decorated shade is old and appropriate but not necessarily original. Foreign burner. 8 1/4 in. McWright collection. $450

236. Blue and yellow lamp with embossed design on base and porcelain shade. Foreign burner. 6 1/4 in. Oldenlite II collection. $300

237. Bisque figural of boy holding a scythe in front of a tree. Foreign burner. Shade missing. 5 3/4 in. McWright collection. $150

238. Bisque figure of a girl holding a sickle and water jug in front of a tree. Foreign burner. Shade missing. 5 3/4 in. McWright collection. $150

239. Bisque lamp with base embossed to resemble basket filled with earth. Trimmed in brown and green. Ball shade shaped to resemble a flower bud about to open; trimmed in white and maroon. Foreign. 6 in. Also found with handle on base. McWright collection. $425

240. White porcelain cat sitting on a suitcase holding a folded umbrella. Yellow glass eyes. Acid etched shade. 11 in. Author's collection. $450(Note: This lamp also found in a larger size, approximately 20 in.)

241. White porcelain cat with blue ribbon around the neck. Tail curled around front leg. Yellow glass eyes. White Bristol shade. 11 in. Author's collection. $450

242. Porcelain owl base with yellow glass eyes and beak. Yellow umbrella shade. Foreign burner. 10 in. Author's collection. $500
Note: None of pictured figural lamps have original shades. It is not known for certain that any shade was specifically designed for only one base. Shades were sold individually.

243. Porcelain base with applied flowers and cherub figure. Blue ground with gold highlighting. Multicolored floral decoration on the shade. Victor burner. 11 in. Knox collection. $550

244. White bisque font held by three blue-chested cherubs. Dark brown foot. Blue satin shade with white enameled floral decor. The shade is old and appropriate but not necessarily original. Foreign burner. 7 7/8 in. McWright collection. $450

245. Blue bisque font held by three pink breasted cherubs. Straw colored foot. Pink satin shade with white enameled floral decor. The shade is old and appropriate but not necessarily original. Nutmeg burner. 8 1/8 in. McWright collection. $450

246. Bisque clowns (2) playing with a balloon executed in pastel blue, pink and yellow. Gold and white beaded trim. Blue cased ball shade. Foreign burner. 12 1/2 in. Also found with a pink cased shade. McWright collection. $600

247. All white sitting kitten. Foreign burner. 3 1/2 in. Ruf collection. $250

248. Majolica-type handled Toby lamp. Acorn burner. 3 1/2 in. Ruf collection. $250

249. White cat sitting on brown pillow. Milk glass shade. 8 1/2 in. Ruf collection. $250

Opposite page, bottom:

250. Raised flowers on egg shaped font depicting emerging pig next to reclining boy's shoulder. Milk glass ball shade. Foreign burner. 7 1/4 in. Ruf collection. $300

251. "Black Boy Hooda" riding on a brown porcelain elephant transporting tea basket on colorful pink and flower fringed blanket. Foreign burner. 7 in. Ruf collection. $450

252. White porcelain poodle wearing a pink collar. Yellow glass eyes 6 1/2 inc. Ruf collection. $450

253. Bisque girl standing beside a large vase. Raised flowers and leaves in green, pink and yellow decorate the vase. White chimney shade. Foreign burner. 10 1/2 in. to top of chimney. Ruf collection. $400

254. Porcelain collie dog in natural colors sitting on base marked "EBS." Butterscotch cased umbrella shade. Foreign burner. 13 1/2 in. Ruf collection. $800

255. White porcelain dog with slight brown shading sitting on a base marked "PS." Foreign burner. 8 in. Ruf collection. $450

256. Realistic colored brown porcelain monkey with white collar holding a banana. Base marked "PSL." Reverse painted green and maroon umbrella shade. Foreign burner. 10 3/4 in. Ruf collection. $700

257. China figural boy standing next to a woven font. Colorful design of fired on paint displayed on his trousers; gold outlining bolero and trousers. Foreign burner. 7 in. Author's collection. $200

258. Bisque girl sitting in a basket canopy chair. Dress and shoes are aqua. Aqua satin ball shade. Foreign burner. 9 in. Author's collection. $450

259. China figural base of cherub sitting next to Dresden-type font with colorful pink applied roses and rose colored flowers. Pink cased umbrella shade not original. Nutmeg burner. 8 in. Author's collection. $300

260. Bisque tree trunk in natural colors with branches extended out on both sides. Foreign burner. 5 in. Hornwood collection. $150

261. Figural base of a boy sitting next to a barrel. Foreign burner. 5 in. Hornwood collection. $200

262. Figural base of a reclining cherub holding a large decorated egg. Blue ball shade. Nutmeg burner. 9 in. Hornwood collection. $450

263. Figural base of a girl dressed in pink dress and bonnet standing next to a bee hive. Utilitarian ball shade not original. Foreign burner. 8 1/2 in. Author's collection. $450

264. White china girl standing next to a corn pattern font. White ball shade not original. See Smith Book II #338. Nutmeg burner. 8 in. Author's collection. $250

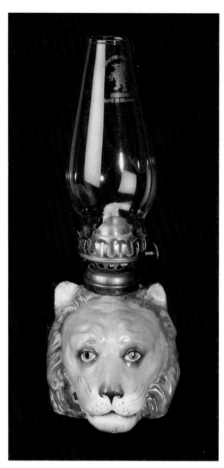

265. Porcelain lion head lamp in natural colors. Bottom of base has blue anchor markings. Foreign burner. 3 1/2 in. Author's collection. $450

266. White porcelain glossy owls head lamp. Yellow glass eyes. Blue anchor mark and impressed "4266" - "E B S" on bottom of base. Hornet burner. 4 in. Solverson collection. $450

267. Porcelain face of a dog peg lamp font. The brass collar on the brass spring peg holder is stamped "Rd 27639" and porcelain portion of the peg is impressed in blue "Rd 23643." Foreign burner. 4 in. from peg to top of collar. Solverson collection. $400

268. Porcelain terrier finger lamp with molded handle in natural colors. Glass eyes and black collar. Hornet burner. 4 1/4 in. Gustin collection. $500

269. White milk glass lamp depicting owl on three sides. White Bristol utilitarian-type shade. Vienna burner. 6 3/4 in. Author's collection. $325

270. Bisque artichoke-type finger lamp with pink rosebuds painted to highlight each leaf. Pink satin chimney with rosebud indentation. Foreign burner. 7 1/4 in. Author's collection. $475

271. White china figural clown in squatting position with blue and red polka dots. White Bristol shade. Vienna burner. 6 3/4 in. Author's collection. $350

272. PAIRPOINT candle lamp in white milk glass with green windmill decor and gold highlighting. Same burner and candle shade as shown in Smith book II #395. 8 3/4 in. Also found with multicolored floral decor with pink or blue candle shades. McWright collection. $950

273. T V Limoge Bristol peg lamp painted with daisy sprays and a gold band on the bottom of the shade and base. Marked "T V, Limoge, France." Acorn burner. 11 in. Oldenlite II collection. $900

274. Brass and porcelain pedestal composite lamp with acid etched ball shade. Font is white opaline. A portion of the stem is pale pink porcelain with tiny white and blue flowers, green leaves. Acorn burner. 10 in. Also see Thuro's Book I page #217. Author's collection. $350

275. Composite stem lamp. Cut and frosted font. Floral decorated white milk glass connector with a black enameled foot. Acorn burner. 6 1/4 in. McWright collection. $250

276. Bisque owl in natural colors. Base of the lamp is a log; shade fits over foreign burner and rests on log base. Green glass eyes; made by Capo de Monte. 5 1/2 in. Author's collection. $7,000

277. Parian owl with base the shape of an owls head; shade has an owl sitting in half moon in 3 places; stars and clouds throughout the shade. Ridged top of shade and bottom of base. Nutmeg burner. 7 1/2 in. Author's collection. $2,500

278. Lime green satinized milk glass lamp. Base has kissing cupids; tiny ball shade. Foreign burner. 5 1/2 in. Wharton collection. $500

279. Colorful Dresden-type figural base with elephant head on either side. Applied flowers in pink with green leaves; fired on painted flowers in pink, yellow and purple. Old snuffer-type burner. "#73" marked on bottom. 5 1/4 in. Author's collection. $225

280. Delft finger lamp with leaf-type handle. Oversized collar with round wick burner. Riser marked "Prima Rundbrunner." 5 in. Author's collection. $200

281. Blue china figural finger lamp of comical man. Gold outlining his collar, mouth, eyes and hat. Burner with snuffer marked "Paris PRF." 4 1/2 in. Author's collection. $350

282. Aqua basket weave base with 2 separate vases sitting on tree trunk. Base marked "Moore Bros." White milk glass shade. P/A Victor burner. 10 1/2 in. Author's collection. $275

283. Royal Worcester cream base with deep pink colored flowers; purple butterfly, brown leaves. Deep pink upturned ruffled shade not original but complimentary to lamp. Foreign burner. 10 in. Author's collection. $600

284. Light blue porcelain base with four different cupid scenes. Gold highlighting each panel. Acid etched shade. Foreign burner. 10 in. Author's collection. $350

285. White porcelain finger lamp with matching ball shade. Pink flowers and green leaves painted throughout. Foreign burner. 10 in. Author's collection. $425

286. Sterling silver base with 3 ridged ball feet. Bristol ball shade with pink roses, green leaves. Burner marked "Made in Germany." 9 1/2 in. Author's collection. $275

287. Bisque figural of girl leaning against a basket weave font. Colors of cream and beige. Cream lined wicker shade. Foreign burner. 10 1/4 in. Authors collection. $350

288. Copper embossed base of cupids driving mule drawn carts. Bristol ball shade with copper colored leaves and pink/purple flowers. Shade not original but complimentary to base. Foreign burner. 10 in. Author's collection. $250

289. White bristol glass decorated lamp with blue bell flowers and green leaves. Shade also bears the phrase "GOD NATT." (Icelandic Goodnight) in black. Foreign burner. 9 1/2 in. McWright collection. $325

290. Milk glass lamp with embossed and painted design on pedestal brass footed base with ball shade. Nutmeg burner. 10 in. Oldenlite II collection. $325

291. Porcelain finger lamp with matching ruffled inverted white milk glass shade. Lavender, green and brown floral decor with gold highlighting. Foreign burner. 7 3/4 in. McWright collection. $425

292. Meissen porcelain base with applied flowers and gold highlighting. Reticulated stem. Blue crossed swords mark. Cherub and festoon multicolored transfer-decorated white milk glass shade. Victor burner. 12 1/4 in. McWright collection. $750

293. White milk glass lamp with delicate multicolored floral decor: maroon and blue highlighting. For-eign burner. 10 in. A variant of Smith Book I #565. McWright collection. $700

294. Two-tier Jr. banquet lamp in white milk glass with aqua and gold floral decor. Square font mounted on a brass foot. Shade is ovoid shaped with a tightly ruffled top edge. Victor burner. 12 3/4 in. McWright collection. $450

295. Embossed white milk glass base with 5 1/2 in. ball shade. Both pieces floral decorated with gold highlighting. Victor burner. 12 in. McWright collection. $350

296. Milk glass banquet sized lamp decorated with yellow shading and pink and blue flowers. P/A Victor burner. 17 1/2 in. Reference name in Consolidated Lamp and Glass Company catalog as "Ionic Princess." Reesbeck collection. $650

297. Milk glass lamp with multi-color floral decoration and gold trim. Kosmos burner. 10 1/4 in. Reesbeck collection. $350

Left:

298. White shading to blue bristol glass lamp with colorful floral and bird decor. Opalescent applied shell feet. Upturned ruffled shade with matching decor. 10 1/2 in. Frenzel collection. $800

Center:

299. Green ground over white Bristol glass. Elaborate gold scroll design throughout base and shade. P/A Victor burner. 10 1/2 in. Author's collection. $500

Right:

300. Pale pink shading to white milk glass lamp decorated with gold butterfly and white flowers. Ruffled upturned shade. Opalescent applied shell feet. Also found in blue. Foreign burner. 10 3/4 in. Lennox/ VanderMeer collection. $675

301. Blue honeycomb pattern lamp. Base is similar to Smith Book I #433 but different in size and design. Upturned lightly flared out shade. Acorn burner. 6 1/2 in. Author's collection. $500

302. Blue opalescent wide panelled lamp with clear applied shell feet. Chimney globe shade is crimped-in then flared-out and ruffled. Foreign burner. 7 1/2 in. Author's collection. $1,600

303. Yellow opalescent wide panelled lamp with clear applied shell feet. Chimney globe shade is crimped-in then flared-out and ruffled the same as preceding lamp. Also found in cranberry. Similar to Smith Book I #514. Foreign burner. 7 1/2 in. Author's collection. $1,600

304. Cranberry Rubina honeycomb pattern lamp with clear applied feet. Upturned lightly flared out shade. Nutmeg burner. 6 1/2 in. Author's collection. $800

305. Blue milk glass shade and base with matching filigree. Similar to Smith Book I #176. Acorn burner. 5 1/2 in. Rosenow collection. $450

306. Vasa Marrhina glass with white background in colors of brown, pink and blue. Flecks of silver mica throughout both pieces. Upturned ruffled shade. Foreign burner. 5 3/4 in. Lennox/VanderMeer collection. $1,800

307. Raspberry satin DQMOP lamp similar to Smith Book I #599. Upturned square ruffled shade. Also found in blue. Foreign burner. 6 in. Solverson collection. $2,200

308. Honey-mustard colored satin glass lamp with rust leaves, green reeds and tiny pink flowers. Ball shade. Foreign burner. 6 1/2 in. Author's collection. $1,200

309. Fireglow lamp in natural color of brownish pink with rust and brown decorations. Dragonfly on shade and base. Variant of Smith Book I #574. Foreign burner. 6 1/2 in. Author's collection. $1,500

310. Pale apricot colored satin glass lamp decorated with olive green leaves and stems; tiny white flowers on base and shade. Foreign burner.   7 in. Author's collection. $1,200

311. Raspberry satin swirled base and shade. Triangular shaped base with beading design at the bottom. Identical beading on the shade. Nutmeg burner. 8 in. Author's collection. $1,300

312. Blue satin raindrop mother-of-pearl lamp with embossed paneled design. Flared out chimney globe shade. Hornet burner. 8 1/2 in. Author's collection. $1,700

313. Raspberry to pink satin glass with embossed design on shade and base. Upturned ruffled butterfly-type shade. Foreign burner. 8 1/2 in. Author's collection. $1,700

314. Chartreuse to white satin embossed shade and base. Upturned ruffled shade. A variant of Smith Book II #517. Nutmeg burner. 8 1/2 inc. $1,300

315. White opalescent lamp with upturned ruffled shade. Foreign burner. 8 1/2 in. Carrey collection. $800

316. White satin glass lamp with slight vertical opalescent swirl pattern in both shade and base Upturned ruffled shade. Foreign burner. 9 in. Similiar to Smith book II #510. Lennox/VanderMeer collection. $800

318. Cranberry pedestal-type lamp with upturned ruffled shade. Foreign burner. 9 1/2 in. Lennox/VanderMeer collection. $875

317. Blue snowflake lamp without the silver filigree as shown in Smith Book I #473. Nutmeg burner. 7 in. Also found in cranberry and white opalescent. Lennox/VanderMeer collection. $900

319. Sapphire blue Mary Gregory-type lamp with white enamel painted child figures on base and ball shade. Foreign burner. 6 1/2 in. Carrey collection. $800

320. Candy-stripe pattern in pink and white cased glass lined white. Chimney globed shade. Hornet burner. 8 1/2 in. Also found in cranberry and clear overshot. Footed version is Smith Book I #548. McWright collection. $850

321. Honey amber glass lamp with opalescent stripes; matching chimney globe shade. Hornet burner. 8 1/4 in. McWright collection. $625

322. Pink and white ribbed swirl lamp in dewdrop design. White cased lining. Chimney globe shade. Similar to Smith Book I #548. Hornet burner. 8 in. White collection. $850

323. Pink candy-stripe reverse swirl cased lamp with clear glass applied feet. Foreign burner. 8 in. Author's collection. $1,600

324. Pink candy-stripe ribbed base and chimney globe shade. Clear glass applied feet. Hornet burner. 9 1/2 in. Author's collection. $1,400

325. Green cased satin glass candy-stripe lamp with frosted feet. Upturned ruffled shade. Similar to Smith Book I #527. Foreign burner marked "R. Ditmar Wien." 7 1/2 in. Author's collection. $1,900

326. Pink candy-stripe lamp with clear applied feet. Umbrella shade. Nutmeg burner. 8 in. Author's collection. $1,500

327. Blue satin mother-of-pearl in the raindrop pattern with applied blue feet. Nutmeg burner. 8 in. Variant of Smith book I #531. McWright collection. $1,900

328. Pink and white cased candy-striped lamp lined in white. Inverted shade with squared candy ribbon on top edge of shade. Five applied crystal shell feet. Foreign burner. 10 in. Knox collection. $2,000

329. End of day lamp in pink, red, green and maroon. Clear glass applied feet. Ribbed and swirled design in base and shade. Foreign burner. 9 in. Oldenlite II collection. $1,800

330. Blue clear glass lamp with pedestal-type base. Upturned ruffled shade. Foreign burner. 7 in. Gustin Collection. $600

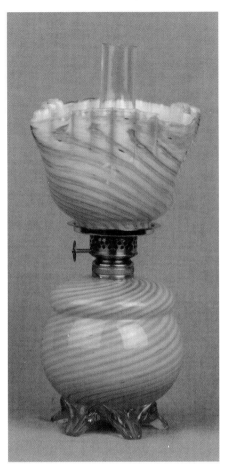

331. Pink and white candy-striped lamp with clear applied feet. Upturned square ruffled shade. Nutmeg burner. 8 in. Author's collection. $1,400

332. Blue to clear panelled lamp. Upturned ruffled shade. Foreign burner. 10 1/2 in. Author's collection. $875

333. Textured glass lamp with hand painted farmhouse scene. Top of shade and base shading to purple. Farm scene in colors of cream, brown, lavender and green. Foreign burner. 7 1/4 in. Author's collection. $1,000
Note: This lamp has the same base but a different shade than the next lamp.

334. Textured lamp with farm scene. French enamel farmhouse design on shade and base. Upturned ruffled shade coloring to lavender at the top. Foreign burner. 7 1/2 in. Carrey collection. $1,200

335. Vaseline opalescent reverse swirl shade and base. Base is flattened on 2 sides. Applied shell feet and butterfly shaped shade. Foreign burner. 8 1/2 in. Author's collection. Note: I pictured both of these lamps to illustrate the fact that in some cases there are two shades for the same identical base. $2,300

336. Honey and butterscotch reverse swirl base and shade. Base is flattened on 2 sides. Pink applied shell feet and ball shade. Foreign burner. See Smith Book I #544. 8 1/2 in. Author's collection. $2,500

337. Aqua opalescent footed lamp with upturned fluted shade and matching chimney. Similar to Smith Book I #517. Foreign burner. 7 in. Author's collection. $1,900

338. Cranberry diamond quilted pattern lamp with clear applied feet. Shade differs from lamp shown in Smith Book I #527. Nutmeg burner. 8 1/2 in. Author's collection. $1,400

339. Light blue opalescent ribbed lamp. Shade has narrow horizontal swirls while the stem base and matching chimney have vertical swirls. Foreign burner. 7 1/4 in. Author's collection. $1,800

340. Amber panelled font with an unusual pedestal-type base and matching amber horizontal ribbed square shade. Foreign burner. 7 in. Rosenow collection. This shade has also been found with a different base and matching ribbed chimney. $900

341. Cased pink opalescent swirled ridged base and shade. Unique pedestal-type base. Upturned 4 sided shade and matching chimney. Foreign burner. 7 1/4 in. Carrey collection. $1,950

342. Cranberry shade and base with swirled design. Base is unique pedestal shape. Upturned ruffled shade and matching chimney. Foreign burner. 7 1/2 in. Carrey collection. $1,800

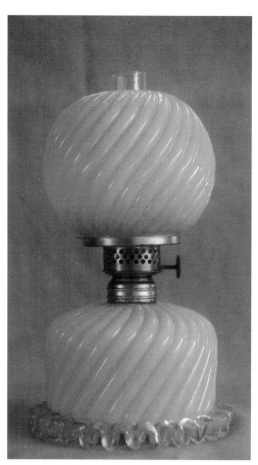

343. Yellow ribbed swirled opaque lamp with clear applied ruffle around bottom of the base. Matching ball shade. Nutmeg burner. 7 in. White collection. $1,500

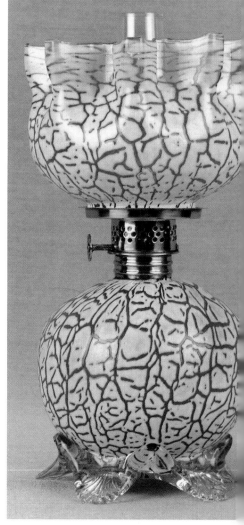

344. Light blue crackle glass with five applied crystal shell feet. Up-turned ruffled shade. Nutmeg burner. 7 3/4 in. McWright collection. $2,000

345. White satin panelled base slightly swirled with matching panelled shade similar to Smith Book II #267. Brown and yellow floral decor with green leaves. Purported to be Pairpoint/Mt. Washington. Nutmeg burner. 7 1/2 in. Bridges collection. $1,100

346. Custard colored lamp with clear applied feet. Base similar to Smith Book II #520. Umbrella shade. Nutmeg burner. 8 in. Author's collection. $1,200

347. Yellowish chartreuse satin glass lamp with conical shaped shade. No decoration but purported to be Webb. Foreign burner. 7 1/2 in. Author's collection. $2,000

348. Chartreuse to clear frosted panelled lamp. Ornamental shell decoration extending upward on applied shell footed base. Umbrella shade. Similar to Smith Book I #536. 8 in. Author's collection. $1,600

349. Pink crackled overlay base and shade. Clear applied feet. Shade is ribbed swirl. Also found in blue. Nutmeg burner. 9 in. Author's collection. $1,800

350. Raspberry cased lamp with veins of silver throughout base and shade. Applied clear glass feet. Upturned ruffled shade. Kosmos Brenner burner. 9 1/4 in. Author's collection. $2,400

351. Raspberry swirl milk glass lamp with medallion design on base. Similar to Smith Book I #547. Umbrella shade. Also found in blue and yellow. Nutmeg burner. 8 1/4 in. Author's collection. $1,500

352. Blue DQMOP footed lamp with upturned fluted shade. Base is dimpled similar to Smith Book I #594 although shade is different but correct. Also found in pink and rose. Foreign burner. 9 1/2 in. Author's collection. $1,800

353. Sterling silver peg lamp base; font and upturned ruffled shade in pink pulled thread design. Also found in aqua. Foreign burner. 10 in. Author's collection. $1,800

354. Vaseline opalescent stripped satin glass lamp. Upturned lightly ruffled shade. Also found in blue. Foreign burner. 9 1/2 in. Author's collection. $900

355. Pink satin glass lamp with filigree base. Lamp is the same as
shown in Smith Book I #394. (Note:
There are numerous lamps with filigree base only i.e. Smith Book I
#176, #385, #388 and #474). Nut-
meg burner. 8 in. Author's collection. $750

356. Blue milk glass ribbed shade
and base. Filigree on both. See
Smith Book I #299. Nutmeg burner.
8 in. Author's collection. $900

357. Deep rose milk glass lamp with
filigree on ribbed shade and base.
See Smith Book I #297. The design
of filigree is quite unique. Nutmeg
burner. 7 1/2 in. Author's collection.
$1,000

358. Gold painted pot metal base embossed with scenes on all four sides. Oil filler cap marked "B & H." Hand painted bristol ball shades in colors of soft green, blue and rust depicting three angelic figures.   9 in. Cotting collection. $550

359. Squatty melon-ribbed silver plated base with English markings on bottom. Peachblow shade with white enamelled flowers and gold scrollwork. Foreign burner. 7 1/4 in. Although the shade is old and authentic, it is not necessarily original. McWright collection. $700

360. Colorful Imari base sitting on ornate brass pedestal. Brass shoulder and burner marked "W&W Kosmos" with round wick. Acid etched shade. 9 1/2 in. Author's collection. $350

361. Lime green Baccarat shade and base similar to Smith Book I #606. Nutmeg burner. 9 1/2 in. Author's collection. $350

362. Cast metal base embossed with large flowers and ridges. Opaque ball shade. foreign burner. 9 1/2 in. Author's collection. $350

363. Brass embossed base. Pink cased DQMOP ruffled shade not original but complimentary to the base. Nutmeg burner. 9 1/2 in. Lennox/VanderMeer collection. $350

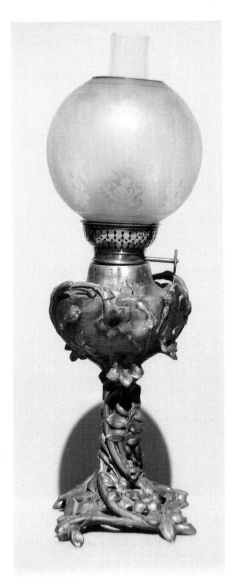

364. Cast metal lamp embossed with floral, leaf and vine design. Acid etched ball shade marked "St. Louis." Foreign burner. 12 1/4 in. Lennox/VanderMeer collection. $375

365. Colorful cloisonne lamp with brass footed stand. Frosted ball shade with gold decorations. Foreign burner. 9 1/2 in. Lennox/VanderMeer collection. $500

366. Silver base marked "Walder & Hall, Sheffield, England #51262." Deep red "Northwoods" Plume shade with white threading. Foreign burner. 10 1/4 in. Oldenlite II collection. $650

367. Silver-plated urn-shaped base with English markings. Ruffled inverted pink opalescent shade is old and appropriate but not necessarily original. Foreign burner. 10 1/4 in. McWright collection. $550

368. Cast zinc (pot metal) base with a frosted iridescent green glass shade adorned with enamelled florals outlined in gold and white. Foreign burner. 9 1/2 in. The shade is old and appropriate but not necessarily original. McWright collection. $450

369. Silver-plated base with engraved design. Frosted ruffled shade in blue and white strip. Foreign burner. 10 1/2 in. Young collection. $500

370. Cylindrical Baccarat swirled rosette pattern base in sapphire blue with an acid-etched floral deco-rated fitterless ball shade. Also Baccarat. Foreign burner. 9 3/4 in. McWright collection. $350

371. Silver-plated base with embossed design. Blue Cameo shade with fern design. Kosmos burner. 9 1/2 in. Young collection. $775

372. Sterling silver base with handles on each side. Blue and white Nailsea shade with ruffled edge. Foreign burner. 11 1/4 in. Author's collection. $550

373. Square brass swirled ribbed base. Pink opalescent swirled shade with ruffling at the top. Foreign burner. 9 3/4 in. Author's collection. $500

374. Sterling silver petal base with stem creating the handle. Same sterling petals form the font. White triangular shaped Nailsea shade with pink outline on top of the shade. Matching Nailsea chimney. Foreign burner. 11 in. to top of chimney. Author's collection. $2,250

375. Clear textured opaque glass lamp with red and blue flowers and green leaves. Brass pedestal base. Foreign burner. 9 1/2 in. Author's collection. $575

376. Pale lavender textured opaque lamp with white metal base decorated with orange leaves and white daisy flowers. Foreign burner. 13 in. Author's collection. $700

377. Clear textured glass lamp with purple and green leaves. Font fits into ornate brass base. Gold outlining upturned fluted shade. Foreign burner. 11 in. Author's collection. $575

378. Pink shading to white cased glass lamp with embossed design in glossy finish. Base mounted on a brass foot. Foreign burner. 12 3/8 in. Also found in blue and yellow with a slightly different foot. McWright collection. $1,000

379. Iridescent green glass peg lamp with gold and enamel painting. Foreign burner. 12 1/2 in. Young collection. $975

380. Yellow cased satin glass lamp with burnt orange blush highlighting on base and shade. Embossed acanthus pattern. Foreign burner. 14 in. Also found in pink, blue and apricot. McWright collection. $1,400

381. Cranberry ribbed and swirled base and shade. Upturned fluted shade. Foreign burner. 10 1/2 in. Hornwood collection. $900

382. Amber irodized lamp with design of flowers and leaves on base and upturned fluted shade. Brass pedestal base. Foreign burner. 12 in. Author's collection. $825

383. Iridescent wine colored pedestal-type lamp with swirl pattern in base and shade. Fringed umbrella shade fits on separated tripod affixed to neck of base; small silver drop-in font. Acorn burner. 12 1/2 in. Author's collection. $1,625

384. Pink crackle overlay lamp with shell feet and shell rigaree around shoulder of base. Upturned ruffled shade. Burner marked "Wien." 9 1/4 in. Author's collection. $2,300

385. Vaseline opalescent vertical stripped lamp with upturned lightly ruffled shade. Foreign burner. 10 1/4 in. Author's collection. $1,875

386. Pink shading to deep raspberry mother-of-pearl lamp. Melon ribbed swirled base and shade. Frosted shell applied feet. Upturned fluted shade. Foreign burner. 11 in. Author's collection. $2,300

387. Vaseline opalescent stripped swirled lamp with applied red splotched pink flowers and vaseline vine on base and shade. Foreign burner. 7 3/4 in. Ruf collection. $1,975

388. Cranberry to clear shade and base. Base has applied shell feet and shell petal on the font. Shade has scalloped top. Nutmeg burner. 8 3/4 in. Ruf collection. $1,450

389. Vaseline opalescent vertical swirled lamp. Upturned lightly fluted shade. Foreign burner. 9 1/2 in. Ruf collection. $1,700

390. Cranberry swirled font and matching shade. Clear glass applied feet and shell rigaree around shoulder of base. Shade is upturned and ruffled. Foreign burner. 8 1/4 in. Ruf collection. $1,500

391. Blue glass lamp with opalescent vertical stripes on shade and base. Applied clear feet. Upturned ruffled shade. Foreign burner. 6 3/4 in. Reesbeck collection. $1,400

392. Cranberry glass lamp with fine optic rib. Inverted shade with a lightly ruffled edge. Five applied crystal shell feet. Foreign burner. 9 in. Knox collection. $1,300

393. Aqua glass lamp with white opalescent vertical stripes on both base and shade. Clear aqua glass applied feet. Foreign burner. 7 1/2 in. Oldenlite II collection. $1,400

394. Iridescent cranberry hobnail lamp with clear applied shell feet. Same shell decoration applied on bottom of base. Umbrella shade fits into ring attached to foreign burner. Similar to Smith Book I #506. 9 1/2 in. Author's collection. $1,200

395. Honey amber glass in a hobnail pattern. Four applied petal feet. Nutmeg burner. 9 in. McWright collection. $1,100

396. Cranberry overshot glass with five applied clear glass petal feet. Umbrella shade. Nutmeg burner. 8 1/4 in. (Also found in green). White collection. $1,900

397. Rubina overshot with vertical ribbing on the base. Clear glass applied shells form the skirt surrounding the base. Upturned scalloped shade. Nutmeg burner. 10 1/4 in. Author's collection. $1,900

398. Cranberry slightly panelled lamp with clear glass rigaree forming a draped wreath around center of the base. Applied shell feet. Upturned ruffled shade. Foreign burner. 9 in. Author's collection. $2,500

399. Rubina overshot lamp with applied shell feet and rigaree around shoulder of base. Upturned tulip shaped shade. Foreign burner. 10 1/2 in. Author's collection. $2,300

400. Rubina Verde crackle glass lamp with applied pink shell feet. Ball-type shade. 10 1/2 in. Author's collection. $3,000

401. Amber shading to pigeon blood panelled lamp. Amber rigaree forming a wreath around center of base. Amber thorn-type applied feet. Upturned scalloped shade. Foreign burner. 9 1/4 in. Author's collection. $2,900

402. Vaseline opalescent stripped lamp with applied shell feet and decoration at bottom of base. Upturned ruffled shade. Foreign burner.   9 1/4 in. Author's collection. $2,900

403. Blue cased marble-type glass lamp. Pedestal base has an applied glass acorn leaf design and clear handle. Upturned ruffled shade. Foreign burner. 9 in. Miller collection. $2,000

404. Pink cased marble-type glass lamp. Base has applied clear glass ridged skirt. Upturned highly ruffled shade. Foreign burner. 9 in. Author's collection. $2,600

405. Pink shading to white satin vertical ribbed base with ball shade. The top of the shade has a crimped ruffle effect. White daisy and green leaves on both pieces. Foreign burner. 10 in. Bridges collection. $2,850

406. Pink cased satin glass lamp. Base is square with block design. Upturned square shade fluted at 4 corners. Foreign burner. 9 1/2 in. Ruf collection. $1,250

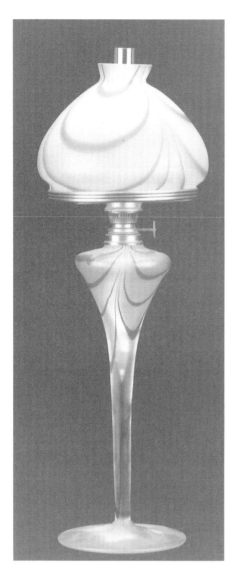

407. Frosted crystal glass with blue loopings pulled through the glass ala Nailsea. Foreign burner. 13 in. (This lamp is a variant of Smith Book I #585). McWright collection. $1,200

408. Green satin shade and a green satin cased base. Bold geometric decor in gold enamel with white Fleur-de-lis. Foreign burner. 14 in. A variant of Smith Book I #585. McWright collection. $1,125

410. Unusual stem lamp. Vaseline decorated stem portion of base with cranberry font. Vaseline ball shade decor matches base. Similar to Smith Book I #584 only larger. Foreign burner. 12 in. Frenzel collection. $2,000

409. Emerald green pedestal lamp with heavy gold decoration on shade and base. Tiny white flowers throughout. Gold outlines scalloped shade. Foreign burner. 10 1/2 in. Author's collection. $1,800

411. Metal base with drop in oil filler. Legs of base are black iron while font is red colored brass. Brass oil filler cap and burner flame spreader both marked B & H. Bristol ball shade highly decorated in shades of red, blue and gold. 12 1/2 in. Cotting collection. $350

412. Cranberry Nailsea font and shade. Embossed brass base. Up-turned ruffled shade. Sometimes referred to as Verre Moire. Foreign burner. 11 1/2 in. Solverson collection. $2,000

413. White Nailsea shade and base with cranberry threading on bottom of base. Upturned ruffled shade with the same cranberry threading. Foreign burner. 13 1/4 in. Ruf collection. $3,000

414. Blue quilted pattern shade and base. Clear glass applied shell feet. Upturned fluted shade. Foreign burner. 10 1/2 in. Ruf collection. $1,000

415. Three piece cased satin glass lamp shading from raspberry to light pink. Ruffled saucer base has 3 frosted feet. Upturned ruffled shade. Foreign burner. 12 in. Ruf collection. $5,000

Below:

416. Cranberry inverted thumbprint lamp with 3 applied glass feet. Ball-type shade and matching chimney. Foreign burner. 7 1/4 in. Miller collection. $1,350

417. Cranberry pulled thread glass lamp with clear applied glass handle and shell feet. Matching upturned shade and chimney. Foreign burner. 7 in. Miller collection. $2,250

418. Blue satin cut velvet diamond pattern. Upturned ruffled shade. Nutmeg burner. 7 in. Miller collection. $2,800

419. Yellow, pink and orange spatter glass lamp with clear glass applied skirt. Upturned ruffled shade. Nutmeg burner. 6 3/4 in. Miller collection. $2,200

Above:

420. Sapphire blue inverted thumbprint pattern lamp with applied shell feet. Upturned ruffled shade. Foreign burner. 9 in. Miller collection. $1,600

421. Raspberry ribbed cased glass lamp with shell petal skirt and rigaree around shoulder of base . Lines of blue and white scattered throughout shade and base. Upturned ruffled shade. Foreign burner. 10 1/2 in. Miller collection. $4,000

422. Yellow Nailsea lamp with frosted applied feet. Upturned ruffled shade. Foreign burner. 11 in. Miller collection. $3,500

423. Blue satin raindrop mother-of-pearl ribbed lamp. Frosted shell skirt and rigaree around shoulder of base. Upturned ruffled shade. See Smith Book I Fig. V. Foreign burner. 9 1/2 in. Author's collection. $3,500

424. Apricot shading to pink mother-of-pearl lamp. Swirled ribbing in shade and base. Frosted applied feet. Upturned ruffled shade. Foreign burner. 10 in. Author's collection. $3,500

425. Blue DQMOP vertical ribbed lamp. Frosted shells form a skirt around the base and shoulder of base. Upturned ruffled shade. Foreign burner. 9 1/2 in. Author's collection. $3,200

426. Mother-of-pearl satin glass in pink and blue with double rows of applied frosted shells at top and bottom of base. Foreign burner. 9 in. Variant of Smith Book II figure XI. Knox collection. $3,500

427. Medium blue cased satin glass shading to a lighter blue. Frosted crystal feet. Ruffled top edge of shade. Foreign burner. 11 1/2 in. Variant of Smith book I #377. Also found in yellow. McWright collection. $1,525

428. Rainbow mother-of-pearl diamond quilted with upturned fluted shade. The font fits into a silver embossed challis. Foreign burner. 10 1/4 in. Author's collection. $3,500

429. Junior size "Tiffany Favrile" lamp. Oval globular shade and font of "Favrile" glass in opal and gold background with gold pulled feather motif. Bronze font insert signed "Tiffany Studio's N.Y. — TG & D Co. D680." Shade is signed "L.C.T. — S-4252." 11 1/2 in. Solverson collection. $5,000

430. Green "Aventurine" glass lamp. The base and shade have a design of gold tracery with white enamel borders highlighting the tracery. Cast brass footed base. Umbrella shade. Foreign burner. 13 in. Solverson collection. $900

431. Cased glass lamp; green cut to clear Cameo. Clear background etched and irodized. Green outer design decorated with gold. Removable brass font. P/A Victor burner. 10 1/2 in. Signed Honesdale. (Honesdale Decorating Co. was the decorating subsidiary of Dorflinger). Reesbeck collection. $2,500

432. Blue Webb cameo lamp with white floral and leaf design. Conical shaped shade. Foreign burner marked "Silber Light Comp." 9 in. Solverson collection. $8,500

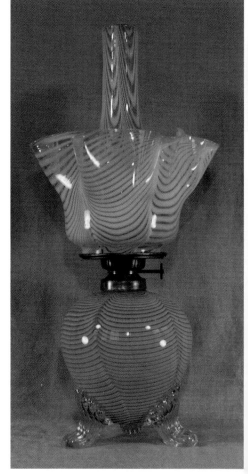

433. Light cranberry and white Verre Moire (Nailsea) lamp with 3 clear applied feet. Upturned fluted shade and matching chimney. Foreign burner. 11 1/4 in. Solverson collection. $4,000

434. Webb Peachblow lamp with 3 frosted applied feet on short squatty base. Conical shaped shade. Foreign burner. 9 in. Carrey collection. $3,000

435. Acid etched Burmese trifooted lamp with colorful rust leaves, acorns and green foliage. Umbrella shade has slight flare at the top. Foreign burner. 9 1/2 in. Attributable to Thomas Webb. Bridges collection. $7,000

436. Nailsea lamp in two-tone pink and frosted crystal glass. Base shaped like a Nautilus shell standing on edge, supported by four frosted, applied feet. Inverted ruffled shade. Foreign burner. 8 1/2 in. (Probably Stevens & Williams). McWright collection. $6,000

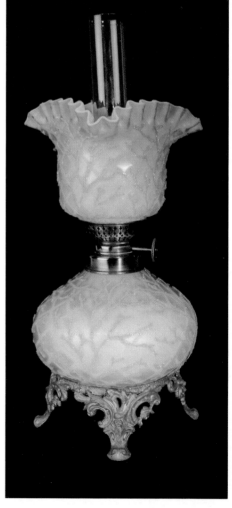

437. Blue to white DQMOP satin glass lamp decorated with coralene seaweed pattern. Ornate brass footed base. Upturned ruffled shade. Bottom of base marked "PATENT." Believed to be Thomas Webb. Foreign burner. 9 1/2 in. Author's collection. $5,000

438. Three piece lamp of blue Nailsea with ruffled saucer base. Ruffled shade and matching chimney fit into unique shade holder and foreign burner. (Probably Stevens & Williams). 14 in. Carrey collection. $5,000

439. Pink cased lamp with three layers of glass; white lining pink and clear glass outside with raised "thorn" in clear glass. Clear glass applied handle and footed base. Scalloped edge at top of shade. Attributable to Stevens and Williams. 7 1/2 in. Hornet burner. Oldenlite II collection. $2,600

440. Webb acid Burmese lamp decorated with yellow acorns and fall colored oak leaves on base and shade. Foreign burner. 6 in. Author's collection. $8,000

441. Midnight blue Webb cameo lamp with white fuschia glory and leaf design. Butterfly not visible. Three frosted applied feet. This lamp is pictured in Ray and Lee Grovernors' English Cameo Glass book page #119. Foreign burner. 7 3/4 in. Author's collection. $15,000

442. Tri-colored Webb cameo lamp, citron with white to pink flowers and leaves. Butterfly not visible. Three frosted applied feet. The scalloped shade is frequently used in Webb lamps. See Smith Book I #610. Foreign burner. 7 1/2 in. Author's collection. $15,000

Bibliography

Grover, Ray and Lee. *English Cameo Glass.* Crown Publishing Company: New York, NY.

Smith, Frank R. and Ruth E. *Miniature Lamps,* 1978. Schiffer Publishing Ltd.: Atglen, PA.

Smith, Ruth. *Miniature Lamps II,* 1982. Schiffer Publishing Ltd.: Atglen, PA.

Solverson, John F. *Those Fascinating Lamps,* 1988. Antique Publications: Marietta, OH.

Solverson, John F. *Value Guide for Miniature Lamps,* 1994-1995.

Thuro, Catherine M.V. *Oil Lamps,* 1976. Wallace Homestead Book Co.: Des Moines, IA.

Thuro, Catherine M.V. *Oil Lamps II,* 1983. Wallace Homestead Book Co.: Des Moines, IA.

Index to Lamp Varieties